Made Easy Slow Cooker Recipes Book

Delicious Meals With Colorful Pictures

By Olivia Anderson

Copyright © by Olivia Anderson

Introduction

Welcome to "Made Easy Slow Cooker Recipes" by Olivia Anderson, a comprehensive guide to transform your cooking experience.

Whether you're a cooking novice or an experienced chef, this book is designed to take your culinary skills to another level. With over 100 diverse, delicious, and easy-to-follow slow cooker recipes, it offers an array of meals that cater to various tastes and dietary preferences. You will find comfort in familiar recipes and excitement in the unfamiliar ones, all crafted to provide an enjoyable, easy, and wholesome cooking experience.

Each recipe in this book has been carefully curated, tested, and perfected by Olivia Anderson, a devoted cook passionate about creating inviting and easy-to-make meals. Olivia shares her most-loved slow cooker recipes in this collection, from succulent meat dishes to hearty vegetarian options, ensuring something for everyone.

Apart from providing detailed step-by-step instructions, "Made Easy Slow Cooker Recipes" offers valuable tips, tricks, and information on how to make the most of your slow cooker. This includes guidance on selecting the right ingredients, suggestions on how to adapt these recipes to suit your taste buds, and much more.

Settle in and get ready to embark on a sensational culinary journey that will make slow-cooking a cherished

Table of Contents

Chapter 1: Sunny Morning Breakfasts

01: Tasty Baked Apples Stuffed

Indulge in a delightful breakfast experience with these baked apples filled with creamy cheese, enhanced by the cozy aromas of cinnamon, nuts, and honey. This recipe combines natural sweetness with a creamy texture, making it a fantastic way to start your day.

Servings: 4

Prepping Time: 15 minutes

Cook Time: 2 hours

Difficulty: Easy

Ingredients:

- 4 large apples
- 1 cup cream cheese, softened
- 2 tbsp honey
- 1/4 cup mixed nuts (like walnuts and almonds), chopped
- 1 tsp cinnamon

➢ Pinch of salt

Step-by-Step Preparation:

1. Core the apples, creating a pocket without cutting all the way through.
2. Combine cream cheese, honey, nuts, cinnamon, and salt in a mixing bowl.
3. Stuff each apple with the cream cheese mixture.
4. Place the stuffed apples in the slow cooker.
5. Cover and cook on low for 2 hours or until apples are tender.

Nutritional Facts: (Per serving)

❖ Calories: 290
❖ Carbohydrates: 36g
❖ Protein: 4g
❖ Fat: 15g
❖ Saturated Fat: 8g
❖ Fiber: 5g
❖ Sugars: 27g

Revel in these baked apples' creamy, nutty, and spicy flavors as you start your day. Perfectly tender apples paired with the richness of cream cheese and the crunchy surprise of nuts make every bite worth the wait. This is breakfast reimagined, proving that healthy can be incredibly tasty, too.

02: Portion of Frittata

Enjoy a savory start to your day with this delectable slow-cooked frittata. It's a breakfast sure to fuel your morning and keep you satisfied.

Servings: 4

Prepping Time: 15 minutes

Cook Time: 2 hours

Difficulty: Easy

Ingredients:

- ➤ 8 large eggs
- ➤ 1 cup fresh spinach, chopped
- ➤ 1 cup mushrooms, sliced
- ➤ 1/4 cup milk
- ➤ Salt and pepper to taste
- ➤ 1/2 cup grated cheese (optional)
- ➤ 1 tablespoon olive oil

Step-by-Step Preparation:

1. Whisk together eggs, milk, salt, and pepper in a bowl.

2. Heat olive oil in a pan and sauté mushrooms until softened.
3. Add spinach to the pan and cook until wilted.
4. Combine the sautéed vegetables with the egg mixture.
5. Pour the mixture into the slow cooker.
6. Sprinkle with cheese if using.
7. Cover and cook on low for 2 hours or until the frittata is set.

Nutritional Facts: (Per serving)

- ❖ Calories: 210
- ❖ Protein: 16g
- ❖ Carbohydrates: 3g
- ❖ Fat: 15g
- ❖ Cholesterol: 375mg
- ❖ Sodium: 180mg
- ❖ Fiber: 1g

A perfect breakfast for busy mornings or leisurely weekends, this slow-cooked frittata melds rich flavors for a heartwarming dish. Enjoy a slice with your favorite hot beverage and start your day on a wholesome note.

03: Oatmeal Porridge

Start your day with a heartwarming bowl of oatmeal porridge. This slow cooker breakfast is drizzled with a delectable caramel sauce that'll make your mornings delightful.

Servings: 4

Prepping Time: 10 minutes

Cook Time: 3 hours

Difficulty: Easy

Ingredients:

> - 1 cup rolled oats
> - 3 cups almond milk
> - 2 ripe bananas, sliced
> - 1 cup blueberries
> - 1/4 cup chopped almonds
> - 1/4 cup shredded coconut
> - 1/2 cup caramel sauce
> - Pinch of salt

Step-by-Step Preparation:

1. Combine rolled oats, almond milk, and a pinch of salt in the slow cooker.
2. Cook on low for 2.5 to 3 hours or until the oats are soft.
3. Stir in sliced bananas and blueberries.
4. Serve in bowls. Top with chopped almonds, shredded coconut, and a generous drizzle of caramel sauce.

Nutritional Facts: (Per serving)

- ❖ Calories: 350
- ❖ Protein: 8g
- ❖ Carbohydrates: 60g
- ❖ Dietary Fiber: 7g
- ❖ Sugars: 20g
- ❖ Fat: 9g
- ❖ Sodium: 75mg

Revel in the creamy texture and rich flavors of this oatmeal porridge. A perfect balance of health and indulgence, it's a breakfast dish to energize and satisfy. Whether you're prepping for a busy day or a leisurely morning, this recipe offers a comforting embrace in every bite.

04: Bread Pudding

Indulge in the warm and comforting flavors of this Bread Pudding with Raisins and Orange Juice. This classic dessert-turned-breakfast delicacy will leave your taste buds craving for more. Perfect for relaxed mornings, it's a delightful combination of soft bread, sweet raisins, and the tang of orange.

Servings: 4

Prepping Time: 15 minutes

Cook Time: 3 hours

Difficulty: Easy

Ingredients:

- 4 cups of stale bread, cubed
- 2 cups of milk
- 3 large eggs
- 3/4 cup of granulated sugar
- 1/2 cup of raisins
- 1/4 cup of fresh orange juice
- 1 teaspoon of vanilla extract
- Zest one orange

➢ 1/4 teaspoon of salt
➢ 1/4 teaspoon of ground cinnamon

Step-by-Step Preparation:

1. Whisk together milk, eggs, sugar, orange juice, and vanilla extract in a mixing bowl until well combined.
2. Stir in the bread cubes, ensuring they are well-soaked.
3. Add raisins, orange zest, salt, and cinnamon to the mixture and gently fold.
4. Pour the mixture into the slow cooker.
5. Set the slow cooker on low and cook for 3 hours or until the pudding is set.
6. Serve warm with your favorite toppings.

Nutritional Facts: (Per serving)

❖ Calories: 385 kcal
❖ Protein: 9g
❖ Carbohydrates: 72g
❖ Fat: 7g
❖ Sugars: 49g
❖ Sodium: 320mg

Round off your morning with this aromatic Bread Pudding with Raisins and Orange Juice. It's delicious and easy to make, giving you a leisurely start to your day. Pair it with freshly brewed coffee or tea for a breakfast experience.

05: French Onion Cheese Quiche

A delightful blend of caramelized onions, melty cheese, and fresh parsley, this French onion cheese quiche is an ideal breakfast treat. Using a slow cooker means waking up to a delicious and savory aroma while adding a grater ensures perfectly textured ingredients.

Servings: 6

Prepping Time: 20 minutes

Cook Time: 3 hours

Difficulty: Intermediate

Ingredients:

> - 2 large onions, thinly sliced
> - 1 cup grated Gruyère cheese
> - 1 cup heavy cream
> - 4 large eggs
> - 1/4 cup fresh parsley, chopped
> - 1 pre-made pie crust
> - 2 tbsp butter
> - Salt and pepper to taste

Step-by-Step Preparation:

1. In a skillet, melt butter and sauté onions until caramelized. Set aside.
2. Whisk together eggs, heavy cream, salt, and pepper in a bowl.
3. Spread the pie crust in the slow cooker, pressing it to fit.
4. Spread the caramelized onions over the crust.
5. Pour the egg mixture over the onions.
6. Top with grated Gruyère cheese.
7. Sprinkle with fresh parsley.
8. Cook on low for 3 hours or until the center is set.

Nutritional Facts: (Per serving):

- ❖ Calories: 350
- ❖ Protein: 12g
- ❖ Carbs: 22g
- ❖ Fat: 24g
- ❖ Fiber: 1g
- ❖ Sugars: 3g
- ❖ Sodium: 320mg

This French onion cheese quiche, enriched with the essence of parsley and masterfully slow-cooked to perfection, promises a gourmet start to your day. Whether for a special brunch or an everyday treat, its rich layers and aromatic warmth make it a must-try for those who relish a savory breakfast. Remember the grater for that perfect cheese texture!

06: Peanut Butter French Toasts

Indulge in a delightful twist to your morning routine with this luscious Peanut Butter French Toast. Drizzled with melted peanut butter and adorned with banana slices, every bite promises a symphony of flavors.

Servings: 4

Prepping Time: 15 minutes

Cook Time: 2 hours

Difficulty: Easy

Ingredients:

> ➤ 8 slices of bread
> ➤ 4 tablespoons of creamy peanut butter
> ➤ 2 bananas, sliced
> ➤ 4 eggs
> ➤ 1 cup milk
> ➤ 1 teaspoon vanilla extract
> ➤ 1/2 teaspoon cinnamon
> ➤ 1/4 cup powdered sugar for garnish

Step-by-Step Preparation:

1. Whisk together eggs, milk, vanilla, and cinnamon in a bowl.
2. Spread peanut butter on one side of each bread slice.
3. Place the bread, peanut butter side up, in the slow cooker.
4. Pour the egg mixture over the bread, ensuring each piece is soaked.
5. Cover and cook on low for 2 to 2.5 hours.
6. Serve with banana slices and a sprinkle of powdered sugar on top.

Nutritional Facts: (Per serving)

❖ Calories: 380
❖ Protein: 15g
❖ Carbs: 48g
❖ Fat: 15g
❖ Fiber: 5g
❖ Sugar: 20g

Conclude your breakfast extravaganza with this delectable treat. Perfectly balanced with the creaminess of peanut butter, the sweetness of bananas, and the delicate touch of powdered sugar, these French toasts are a morning delight worthy of any special occasion or just a pampering weekend morning.

07: Sausage Casserole

Warm up your mornings with this hearty sausage casserole infused with the earthiness of onion leeks and a hint of apple sweetness. Perfectly designed for slow cooker breakfasts, this dish promises a delightful burst of flavors to kick-start your day.

Servings: 4-6

Prepping Time: 15 minutes

Cook Time: 6 hours

Difficulty: Easy

Ingredients:

> ➢ 6 large sausages, pre-cooked
> ➢ 2 onion leeks, sliced
> ➢ 1 apple, cored and chopped
> ➢ 1 cup of chicken broth
> ➢ 2 cloves garlic, minced
> ➢ 1 teaspoon of salt
> ➢ 1/2 teaspoon of black pepper
> ➢ 1 teaspoon of thyme

Step-by-Step Preparation:

1. Place the pre-cooked sausages at the bottom of the slow cooker.
2. Add the sliced onion, leeks, and chopped apple over the links.
3. Mix chicken broth, garlic, salt, pepper, and thyme in a bowl. Pour this mixture into the slow cooker.
4. Set the slow cooker to low and let it cook for 6 hours.
5. Before serving, please give it a gentle stir to mix all flavors.

Nutritional Facts: (Per serving)

- ❖ Calories: 280
- ❖ Protein: 14g
- ❖ Carbohydrates: 20g
- ❖ Fat: 16g
- ❖ Fiber: 2g
- ❖ Sodium: 720mg

Dive into a delectable amalgamation of succulent sausages, crunchy leeks, and the mild sweetness of apple. This sausage casserole is not just a breakfast; it's an experience. Relish each bite and let the flavors transport you to culinary heaven, perfect for lazy weekend mornings or a unique brunch.

08: Maple Pecan Puff Pastry

Indulge in a decadent morning treat with our Maple Pecan Puff Pastry Isolated. These Danish plaits are a delightful fusion of flaky puff pastry, rich maple syrup, and crunchy pecan nuts, perfect for a luxurious breakfast or brunch.

Servings: 6

Prepping Time: 20 minutes

Cook Time: 2 hours 30 minutes

Difficulty: Medium

Ingredients:

> ➤ 2 sheets of ready-made puff pastry
> ➤ 1 cup pecan nuts, roughly chopped
> ➤ 1/2 cup maple syrup
> ➤ 1 egg (for egg wash)
> ➤ 1 tsp vanilla extract
> ➤ A pinch of salt

Step-by-Step Preparation:

1. Lay out the puff pastry sheets and allow them to be at room temperature.
2. Mix the pecan nuts, maple syrup, vanilla extract, and salt in a bowl.
3. Spread the pecan mixture evenly over one sheet of pastry.
4. Place the second pastry sheet on top and cut into six plaits.
5. Transfer the plaits to the slow cooker.
6. Brush the tops with egg wash for a golden finish.
7. Cover and cook on low for 2 hours 30 minutes or until the pastries are puffed and golden.
8. Serve warm.

Nutritional Facts: (Per serving):

- ❖ Calories: 385
- ❖ Fat: 24g
- ❖ Carbohydrates: 35g
- ❖ Protein: 5g
- ❖ Sugar: 15g
- ❖ Sodium: 150mg

Elevate your morning with these delightful Maple Pecan Puff Pastry Isolated. Perfectly flaky and dripping with sweet maple goodness, these pastries will surely be the highlight of your breakfast spread. It is best enjoyed with coffee or tea and shared with loved ones.

09: Chorizo Burrito With Eggs

Savor the richness of chorizo blended with the softness of eggs and potatoes; all encased in a warm burrito wrap. This slow-cooked breakfast delight with a splash of salsa is bound to energize your mornings.

Servings: 4

Prepping Time: 20 minutes

Cook Time: 6 hours

Difficulty: Easy

Ingredients:

> ➢ 1/2 pound chorizo sausage, crumbled
> ➢ 6 large eggs, beaten
> ➢ 2 medium potatoes, diced
> ➢ 1 cup salsa
> ➢ 4 large burrito wraps
> ➢ 1/2 cup shredded cheddar cheese
> ➢ 1/4 cup chopped fresh cilantro
> ➢ Salt and pepper, to taste

Step-by-Step Preparation:

1. In a skillet, brown the chorizo sausage and drain excess fat.
2. In the slow cooker, layer the potatoes, followed by the chorizo.
3. Pour beaten eggs over the chorizo and potatoes.
4. Cook on low for 6 hours.
5. Before serving, warm the burrito wraps.
6. Spoon the egg, chorizo, and potato mixture onto each wrap.
7. Top with salsa, cheddar cheese, and cilantro. Fold and serve.

Nutritional Facts: (Per serving)

- ❖ Calories: 480 kcal
- ❖ Protein: 26g
- ❖ Carbohydrates: 42g
- ❖ Dietary Fiber: 3g
- ❖ Sugars: 4g
- ❖ Fat: 24g
- ❖ Saturated Fat: 9g
- ❖ Cholesterol: 330mg
- ❖ Sodium: 830mg

Dive into the flavors of Mexico every morning with this hearty, slow-cooked breakfast. The combination of spicy chorizo, velvety eggs, and crisp potatoes wrapped in a soft burrito is a culinary adventure that'll make waking up the highlight of your day. Enjoy!

10: Casserole With Zucchini

Warm up your mornings with this hearty slow-cooker breakfast casserole. The delightful combination of zucchini, tomato, and beans provides a nutritious start to your day, making it a favorite for both weekdays and relaxed weekends.

Servings: 6

Prepping Time: 15 minutes

Cook Time: 4 hours on low

Difficulty: Easy

Ingredients:

- 3 medium zucchinis, sliced
- 2 large tomatoes, diced
- 1 can (15 oz) white beans, drained and rinsed
- 6 eggs, beaten
- 1 cup shredded cheddar cheese
- 1/2 cup milk
- 1 tsp salt
- 1/2 tsp black pepper

> ➢ 1/2 tsp garlic powder
> ➢ 1/4 cup fresh basil, chopped

Step-by-Step Preparation:

1. In a bowl, combine zucchini, tomatoes, and beans.
2. Whisk together eggs, milk, salt, pepper, and garlic powder in another bowl.
3. Layer the zucchini mixture at the bottom of the slow cooker.
4. Pour the egg mixture over the zucchini mix.
5. Sprinkle with shredded cheese and chopped basil.
6. Cover and cook on low for 4 hours or until set.
7. Let it cool slightly before serving.

Nutritional Facts: (Per serving)

- ❖ Calories: 220
- ❖ Protein: 14g
- ❖ Carbs: 18g
- ❖ Fiber: 4g
- ❖ Sugars: 4g
- ❖ Fat: 10g
- ❖ Sodium: 400mg

This casserole, rich in flavor and nutrients, is bound to be a hit with your family. Whether prepping for a busy day or setting the table for a leisurely brunch, the melded flavors of zucchini, tomato, and beans create a satisfying meal that keeps you fueled. Happy cooking!

Chapter 2: Leisurely Lunch Delights

11: Irish Stew Made With Beef

Steeped in rich Irish beef stew, it is a hearty, comforting dish perfect for those chilly afternoons. Earthy flavors of potatoes, carrots, and aromatic herbs, every bite transports you straight to the Emerald Isle.

Servings: 6

Prepping Time: 20 minutes

Cook Time: 6-8 hours

Difficulty: Easy

Ingredients:

- ➤ 2 lbs beef chuck, cut into 2-inch pieces
- ➤ 4 large potatoes, peeled and cubed
- ➤ 3 carrots, sliced
- ➤ 1 large onion, chopped
- ➤ 3 cloves garlic, minced
- ➤ 4 cups beef broth

- ➢ 2 teaspoons salt
- ➢ 1 teaspoon black pepper
- ➢ 1 teaspoon dried thyme
- ➢ 1 teaspoon dried rosemary
- ➢ 2 tablespoons tomato paste
- ➢ 1 cup peas (optional)

Step-by-Step Preparation:

1. Season beef pieces with salt and pepper.
2. Combine beef, potatoes, carrots, onion, and garlic in the slow cooker.
3. Whisk together beef broth, tomato paste, thyme, and rosemary in a separate bowl. Pour over beef and vegetables in the slow cooker.
4. Cook on low for 6-8 hours until beef is tender and vegetables are cooked.
5. If using, add peas in the last 30 minutes of cooking.
6. Adjust seasoning if necessary before serving.

Nutritional Facts: (Per serving)

- ❖ Calories: 430
- ❖ Protein: 35g
- ❖ Carbohydrates: 40g
- ❖ Dietary Fiber: 7g
- ❖ Sugars: 5g
- ❖ Fat: 15g
- ❖ Saturated Fat: 6g
- ❖ Sodium: 1100mg

Embrace the heartwarming essence of Ireland with this delightful stew. The slow cooker does all the hard work, allowing the flavors to meld beautifully. Whether celebrating St. Patrick's Day or simply in the mood for a robust lunch, this Irish stew promises to satisfy your cravings and warm your soul.

12: Butternut Squash Pumpkin Stuffed

Indulge in autumn's warm and creamy flavors with this slow cooker dish. A delightful combination of sweet butternut squash and savory spinach-ricotta stuffing will surely delight your palate and warm your soul.

Servings: 4

Prepping Time: 20 minutes

Cook Time: 3 hours on low

Difficulty: Easy

Ingredients:

- 1 medium-sized butternut squash pumpkin
- 2 cups fresh spinach, washed and chopped
- 1 cup ricotta cheese
- 1/2 cup grated Parmesan cheese
- 2 garlic cloves, minced
- 1/4 teaspoon nutmeg
- Salt and pepper to taste
- 1 tablespoon olive oil

Step-by-Step Preparation:

1. Slice the top of the butternut squash and scoop out the seeds.
2. Mix spinach, ricotta, Parmesan, garlic, nutmeg, salt, and pepper in a mixing bowl.
3. Stuff the butternut squash with the spinach and ricotta mixture.
4. Drizzle with olive oil.
5. Place in the slow cooker and cook on low for 3 hours or until the squash is tender.
6. Serve warm.

Nutritional Facts: (Per serving)

- ❖ Calories: 250
- ❖ Protein: 12g
- ❖ Carbs: 30g
- ❖ Fat: 10g
- ❖ Fiber: 6g
- ❖ Sugar: 5g

A cozy meal that encapsulates the essence of fall, this dish is perfect for a lazy Sunday lunch or a special gathering. Enjoy the symphony of flavors as they meld together in the slow cooker, offering a comforting and nutritious treat. Perfect with a crisp salad or crusty bread.

13: Baked Taquitos With Chicken

These Baked Taquitos with Chicken and Cheese are a delightful twist to your lunch meal. Using a slow cooker, the chicken becomes tender and flavorful, and when combined with cheese and baked to perfection, these taquitos are irresistibly crunchy and satisfying.

Servings: 4 people

Prepping Time: 20 minutes

Cook Time: 3 hours (slow cooker) + 15 minutes (baking)

Difficulty: Intermediate

Ingredients:

> - 2 boneless, skinless chicken breasts
> - 1 cup salsa
> - 1 tsp ground cumin
> - 1/2 tsp garlic powder
> - 1/4 cup chopped fresh cilantro
> - 1 cup shredded cheddar cheese
> - 8 small flour tortillas
> - Olive oil for brushing

Step-by-Step Preparation:

1. Place chicken breasts in the slow cooker. Pour salsa over, then sprinkle with cumin and garlic powder.
2. Cook on low for 3 hours or until chicken is tender.
3. Remove chicken from the cooker and shred using two forks. Mix in cilantro and cheese.
4. Preheat oven to 400°F (200°C).
5. Lay out tortillas and place a portion of the chicken mixture in the center of each.
6. Roll up tightly and place seam-side down on a baking sheet.
7. Brush with olive oil.
8. Bake for 15 minutes or until golden and crisp.

Nutritional Facts: (Per serving)

- ❖ Calories: 380 kcal
- ❖ Protein: 24g
- ❖ Carbs: 31g
- ❖ Fats: 16g
- ❖ Fiber: 2g
- ❖ Sodium: 720mg

Elevate your lunch game with these baked taquitos, delivering a fusion of tender chicken and melted cheese in every bite. Serve with guacamole or sour cream for a more flavorful experience. These taquitos will surely be a favorite for a weekend treat or a weeknight surprise.

14: Baked Potato With Tomato Beans

Enjoy a heartwarming slow cooker dish that combines the earthiness of baked potatoes with the tang of tomato beans, all crowned with melted cheddar cheese. This recipe is perfect for those seeking a fulfilling lunch with minimal hassle.

Servings: 4

Prepping Time: 15 minutes

Cook Time: 4 hours on high, 8 hours on low

Difficulty: Easy

Ingredients:

- ➢ 4 large russet potatoes, scrubbed clean
- ➢ 1 can (15 oz) tomato beans
- ➢ 1 cup grated cheddar cheese
- ➢ 1 small onion, diced
- ➢ 2 garlic cloves, minced
- ➢ Salt and pepper to taste
- ➢ 1 tablespoon olive oil
- ➢ Fresh parsley (for garnish)

Step-by-Step Preparation:

1. Pierce each potato several times with a fork.
2. Place potatoes in the slow cooker.
3. Mix tomato beans, onion, garlic, salt, and pepper in a medium bowl.
4. Pour the bean mixture over the potatoes.
5. Drizzle with olive oil and cover.
6. Cook high for 4 hours or low for 8 hours until potatoes are tender.
7. Before serving, sprinkle with cheddar cheese and let melt. Garnish with parsley.

Nutritional Facts: (Per serving)

- ❖ Calories: 350
- ❖ Protein: 10g
- ❖ Carbohydrates: 60g
- ❖ Dietary Fiber: 7g
- ❖ Sugars: 4g
- ❖ Fat: 8g
- ❖ Saturated Fat: 4g
- ❖ Sodium: 450mg

The combination of creamy baked potato, rich tomato beans, and velvety cheddar cheese creates a dish that's not just tasty but also nutritious. This slow cooker lunch ensures a warm, hearty meal awaits you, no matter how busy your day.

15: Birria Beef Tacos With Broth

Inspired by the vibrant flavors of Mexico, these Birria Beef Tacos are simmered to perfection in a rich broth, ensuring each bite is succulent and flavorful. This slow-cooked lunch treat promises a culinary experience like no other.

Servings: 6

Prepping Time: 30 minutes

Cook Time: 8 hours

Difficulty: Intermediate

Ingredients:

- 2 lbs beef chuck roast, cut into chunks
- 5 dried guajillo chiles, seeded and soaked
- 3 garlic cloves
- 1 tsp oregano
- 1/2 tsp cumin
- 2 bay leaves
- 4 cups beef broth
- Salt to taste

- ➢ Corn tortillas for serving
- ➢ Fresh cilantro, chopped (optional)
- ➢ Lime wedges for serving

Step-by-Step Preparation:

1. Combine soaked guajillo chiles, garlic, oregano, cumin, and a pinch of salt in a blender. Blend until a smooth paste forms.
2. In a slow cooker, place beef chunks and bay leaves. Pour over the chile paste.
3. Add beef broth to the cooker, ensuring the beef is submerged.
4. Cook on low for 8 hours or until beef is tender.
5. Once cooked, shred the beef inside the slow cooker.
6. Warm tortillas, then fill with shredded beef. Serve with a side of the broth, garnishing with cilantro and lime if desired.

Nutritional Facts: (Per serving)

- ❖ Calories: 450
- ❖ Protein: 35g
- ❖ Carbohydrates: 20g
- ❖ Fat: 25g
- ❖ Sodium: 700mg
- ❖ Fiber: 3g

The fusion of spices, tender beef, and flavorful broth makes these Birria Beef Tacos more than just a meal – they celebrate tradition. Whether hosting a special lunch or seeking comfort on a cold day, these tacos promise to deliver warmth, depth, and an unparalleled taste.

16: Bacon Cheeseburger

Revel in the comforting flavors of this classic pub-style dish right at home. The delightful combination of juicy beef patties, crispy bacon, gooey cheese, and tangy barbecue sauce is bound to be a favorite. Made conveniently in a slow cooker, it's perfect for a hearty weekend lunch.

Servings: 4

Prepping Time: 15 minutes

Cook Time: 4 hours

Difficulty: Moderate

Ingredients:

> ➤ 4 beef patties
> ➤ 8 slices of bacon
> ➤ 4 cheese slices (cheddar or your choice)
> ➤ 1 cup barbecue sauce
> ➤ 4 burger buns
> ➤ 2 cups frozen French fries
> ➤ Salt and pepper to taste
> ➤ Optional toppings: lettuce, tomato, onions

Step-by-Step Preparation:

1. Place beef patties at the bottom of the slow cooker.
2. Drizzle barbecue sauce over the patties.
3. Layer bacon slices on top.
4. Cover and cook on low for 4 hours.
5. About 30 minutes before serving, bake the French fries as per package instructions.
6. Once cooked, assemble your burgers by placing a beef patty on each bun, topping with a cheese slice, bacon, and any optional toppings.
7. Serve burgers with a side of crispy French fries.

Nutritional Facts: (Per serving)

- ❖ Calories: 650
- ❖ Protein: 35g
- ❖ Carbohydrates: 45g
- ❖ Fats: 35g
- ❖ Sodium: 850mg
- ❖ Sugars: 15g

This slow-cooked pub-style bacon cheeseburger with barbecue sauce and French fries is a game-changer for burger lovers. It effortlessly combines convenience with the delightful taste of a hearty pub meal, making it a must-try for everyone. Enjoy it with friends or family, and let the flavors transport you to your favorite local pub.

17: Roasted Rosemary Chicken Breast

This delectable Roasted Rosemary Chicken Breast with Wild Rice Pilaf is the perfect slow cooker lunch. The aromatic rosemary pairs beautifully with the tender chicken, while the wild rice pilaf adds a delightful nutty contrast. Impress your guests or indulge in a gourmet home-cooked meal.

Servings: 4

Prepping Time: 20 minutes

Cook Time: 4 hours on low

Difficulty: Easy

Ingredients:

- ➢ 4 boneless, skinless chicken breasts
- ➢ 2 tbsp fresh rosemary, finely chopped
- ➢ 2 tbsp olive oil
- ➢ Salt and pepper, to taste
- ➢ 1 cup wild rice
- ➢ 2 1/2 cups chicken broth
- ➢ 1/2 cup diced carrots
- ➢ 1/2 cup diced onions

➢ 1/4 cup chopped parsley

Step-by-Step Preparation:

1. Season chicken breasts with rosemary, salt, and pepper, and drizzle with olive oil.
2. Place the chicken in the slow cooker.
3. Mix wild rice, carrots, onions, and parsley in a bowl.
4. Pour the rice mixture around the chicken in the slow cooker.
5. Pour chicken broth over the rice mixture.
6. Cover and cook on low for 4 hours or until the chicken is cooked and the rice is tender.
7. Serve the chicken over the rice pilaf.

Nutritional Facts: (Per serving)

❖ Calories: 350
❖ Protein: 30g
❖ Carbohydrates: 35g
❖ Dietary Fiber: 3g
❖ Sugars: 2g
❖ Fat: 8g
❖ Saturated Fat: 1.5g
❖ Sodium: 600mg

The gentle flavors of rosemary and the earthy tones of the wild rice create a symphony in this dish, offering a wholesome and filling lunch. Whether hosting a luncheon or simply yearning for a nourishing meal, this Roasted Rosemary Chicken Breast with Wild Rice Pilaf is a delightful choice. Savor each bite!

18: Vegan Chili Beans

Warm up your day with a hearty Vegan Chili beans, avocado, and cilantro. This dish offers the perfect spice, texture, and freshness blend, ensuring a satisfying lunchtime delight.

Servings: 4-6

Prepping Time: 15 minutes

Cook Time: 6 hours on low

Difficulty: Easy

Ingredients:

- 2 cans (15 oz) kidney beans, drained and rinsed
- 1 can (15 oz) black beans, drained and rinsed
- 1 can (14.5 oz) diced tomatoes
- 1 large onion, finely chopped
- 2 bell peppers, chopped
- 3 cloves garlic, minced
- 1 tbsp chili powder
- 1 tsp cumin
- Salt and pepper to taste

- ➢ 2 avocados, sliced
- ➢ Fresh cilantro, chopped for garnish

Step-by-Step Preparation:

1. Combine kidney beans, black beans, tomatoes, onion, bell peppers, garlic, chili powder, cumin, salt, and pepper in the slow cooker.
2. Stir well to combine.
3. Cover and cook on low for 6 hours.
4. Once done, ladle chili into bowls.
5. Top each bowl with slices of avocado and sprinkle with fresh cilantro.

Nutritional Facts: (Per serving)

- ❖ Calories: 270 kcal
- ❖ Protein: 10g
- ❖ Carbohydrates: 39g
- ❖ Dietary Fiber: 14g
- ❖ Fats: 9g
- ❖ Sodium: 280mg

This Vegan Chili beans with avocado and cilantro dish encapsulates the essence of a slow-cooked meal, merging deep flavors with refreshing touches. Serve with crusty bread or tortilla chips for an even heartier experience. Enjoy your flavorsome, nutritious lunch that promises both warmth and satisfaction.

19: Barbeque Pulled Pork Sandwich

Savor the ultimate comfort food with this slow-cooked barbeque pulled pork sandwich. This dish promises a burst of flavor in every bite. Ideal for weekend feasts, get ready to be transported to BBQ heaven.

Servings: 4

Prepping Time: 20 minutes

Cook Time: 8 hours

Difficulty: Medium

Ingredients:

> ➢ 2 lbs pork shoulder
> ➢ 1 cup BBQ sauce, plus extra for serving
> ➢ 1/4 cup brown sugar
> ➢ 1 tbsp apple cider vinegar
> ➢ 1 tsp smoked paprika
> ➢ 1 tsp garlic powder
> ➢ 1/4 tsp cayenne pepper
> ➢ 4 burger buns
> ➢ 2 cups frozen fries

➤ Coleslaw (optional for serving)

Step-by-Step Preparation:

1. Mix BBQ sauce, brown sugar, apple cider vinegar, smoked paprika, garlic powder, and cayenne pepper in a bowl.
2. Place the pork shoulder in the slow cooker and pour the sauce mixture over it.
3. Cover and cook on low for 8 hours or until pork is tender.
4. About 30 minutes before serving, bake the frozen fries as per package instructions.
5. Once the pork is done, shred it using two forks and mix it with the sauce in the cooker.
6. Serve pulled pork on burger buns, topped with extra BBQ sauce and, optionally, coleslaw. Pair with crispy fries on the side.

Nutritional Facts: (Per serving):

❖ Calories: 650
❖ Protein: 35g
❖ Carbohydrates: 60g
❖ Dietary Fiber: 5g
❖ Sugars: 20g
❖ Fat: 30g
❖ Saturated Fat: 10g
❖ Sodium: 800mg

A surefire hit for any gathering, this Barbeque Pulled Pork Sandwich offers the perfect smoky, sweet, and savory balance. Enjoy the succulent tenderness of the pork and the crunch of the fries, ensuring a delightful meal with you returning for seconds. Happy feasting!

20: Fettucini Aflredo Pasta With Chicken

Indulge in the creamy allure of this Fettuccini Alfredo Pasta paired with tender chicken and fragrant parsley. This dish offers a harmonious blend of flavors that melt seamlessly into each other, perfect for a mid-day delight.

Servings: 4

Prepping Time: 15 minutes

Cook Time: 4 hours on low

Difficulty: Easy

Ingredients:

> ➤ 8 oz fettuccini pasta
> ➤ 2 chicken breasts, thinly sliced
> ➤ 2 cups heavy cream
> ➤ 1 cup grated Parmesan cheese
> ➤ 4 cloves garlic, minced
> ➤ 2 tbsp butter
> ➤ 1/4 cup chopped fresh parsley
> ➤ Salt and pepper to taste

Step-by-Step Preparation:

1. Place the chicken, heavy cream, garlic, butter, salt, and pepper in the slow cooker. Mix well.
2. Cover and cook on low for 3-4 hours or until the chicken is fully cooked.
3. About 30 minutes before serving, cook the fettuccini according to package instructions.
4. Stir the cooked fettuccini and Parmesan cheese into the slow cooker.
5. Garnish with chopped parsley before serving.

Nutritional Facts: (Per serving)

- ❖ Calories: 650
- ❖ Protein: 35g
- ❖ Carbs: 45g
- ❖ Fat: 35g
- ❖ Sodium: 480mg
- ❖ Sugar: 2g

Relish the comfort of home-cooked Fettuccini Alfredo, enhanced by the chicken's juiciness and the parsley's freshness. This slow-cooked sensation promises a meal that fills the stomach and warms the heart. Every bite is a creamy embrace of pure gastronomic joy, perfect for gatherings or a family weekend.

21: Traditional Lasagna

This traditional lasagna with bolognese sauce and basil leaves is the ultimate comfort food, brought to life in your slow cooker. A perfect blend of flavors and textures, it promises to be a showstopper at your dinner table.

Servings: 6

Prepping Time: 20 minutes

Cook Time: 4 hours

Difficulty: Intermediate

Ingredients:

- 12 lasagna noodles, uncooked
- 1 lb ground beef
- 1 jar (24 oz) marinara sauce
- 1 cup bolognese sauce
- 2 cups ricotta cheese
- 2 cups shredded mozzarella cheese

- ➢ 1/2 cup grated Parmesan cheese
- ➢ 1 egg
- ➢ 2 tbsp olive oil
- ➢ 1/2 cup chopped fresh basil leaves
- ➢ 1 tsp salt
- ➢ 1/2 tsp black pepper

Step-by-Step Preparation:

1. In a skillet, brown the ground beef with olive oil. Drain excess fat and mix with marinara and bolognese sauce.
2. Combine ricotta cheese, 1 cup mozzarella, Parmesan cheese, egg, salt, and pepper in a separate bowl.
3. Lay a few lasagna noodles at the bottom of the slow cooker.
4. Spread a layer of the beef and sauce mixture, followed by the cheese mixture.
5. Repeat layers until all ingredients are used up, ending with sauce and cheese on top.
6. Cover and cook on low for 4 hours.
7. 10 minutes before serving, sprinkle the remaining mozzarella and basil leaves on top.
8. Serve warm and enjoy!

Nutritional Facts: (Per serving)

- ❖ Calories: 480
- ❖ Total Fat: 20g
- ❖ Saturated Fat: 9g
- ❖ Cholesterol: 60mg
- ❖ Sodium: 820mg
- ❖ Total Carbohydrates: 50g
- ❖ Dietary Fiber: 4g
- ❖ Sugars: 8g
- ❖ Protein: 25g

Savor the rich layers of this slow-cooked lasagna, melding bolognese sauce with a symphony of cheeses and fresh basil. This meal not only warms your stomach but also your heart, making every dinner moment truly special. Serve with a fresh salad or crusty bread for the perfect Italian feast.

22: BBQ Beef Rib

Succulent and flavorful, BBQ beef ribs are an absolute delight for those who appreciate the rich essence of slow-cooked meat. This slow cooker recipe ensures that every bite is tender and dripping with barbecue goodness.

Servings: 4-6 people

Prepping Time: 20 minutes

Cook Time: 8 hours

Difficulty: Easy

Ingredients:

> - 4 lbs beef ribs
> - 1 cup barbecue sauce
> - 2 tablespoons brown sugar
> - 1 tablespoon paprika
> - 2 teaspoons garlic powder
> - 1 teaspoon onion powder
> - 1 teaspoon black pepper
> - 1/2 teaspoon salt
> - 1/4 cup apple cider vinegar

> ➢ 1/2 cup beef broth

Step-by-Step Preparation:

1. Mix brown sugar, paprika, garlic powder, onion powder, pepper, and salt in a bowl to prepare the rub.
2. Generously coat the beef ribs with the rub.
3. Place the ribs in the slow cooker.
4. Combine barbecue sauce, apple cider vinegar, and beef broth. Pour the mixture over the ribs.
5. Cover and cook on low for 8 hours or until ribs are tender.
6. Once cooked, transfer ribs to a platter and drizzle with the cooking liquid from the slow cooker.

Nutritional Facts: (Per serving)

- ❖ Calories: 680 kcal
- ❖ Protein: 40g
- ❖ Fat: 45g
- ❖ Carbohydrates: 30g
- ❖ Fiber: 1g
- ❖ Sugar: 25g
- ❖ Sodium: 780mg

The essence of slow cooking truly shines in this BBQ Beef Rib recipe, making it a must-try for every meat lover. It's the perfect blend of savory flavors with the ease of a slow cooker method. So, set it, forget it, and return to an irresistible dinner that will leave you craving more. Enjoy!

23: Moroccan Chicken Tagine

Moroccan chicken tagine is an exotic dish that transports your taste buds to North Africa. Fragrant spices, olives, and salted lemons meld in a slow cooker, resulting in a tantalizingly tender and flavorful chicken masterpiece.

Servings: 6

Prepping Time: 20 minutes

Cook Time: 4 hours on low

Difficulty: Intermediate

Ingredients:

- 6 bone-in, skin-on chicken thighs
- 2 salted lemons, thinly sliced
- 1 cup pitted green olives
- 2 onions, finely chopped
- 3 garlic cloves, minced
- 2 tsp ground cumin
- 1 tsp ground ginger
- 1 tsp ground turmeric
- 1/2 tsp saffron threads

- ➢ 2 cups chicken broth
- ➢ Fresh cilantro, chopped, for garnish
- ➢ 3 tbsp olive oil
- ➢ Salt and pepper to taste

Step-by-Step Preparation:

1. Heat olive oil and brown chicken thighs on both sides in a large skillet. Remove and set aside.
2. In the same skillet, sauté onions and garlic until translucent.
3. Add cumin, ginger, turmeric, and saffron. Cook for 2 minutes, stirring frequently.
4. Transfer the onion-spice mixture to the slow cooker. Add chicken, salted lemons, olives, and chicken broth.
5. Cook on low for 4 hours or until chicken is tender.
6. Garnish with fresh cilantro before serving.

Nutritional Facts: (Per serving)

- ❖ Calories: 350
- ❖ Protein: 28g
- ❖ Carbohydrates: 12g
- ❖ Dietary Fiber: 2g
- ❖ Sugars: 3g
- ❖ Fat: 22g
- ❖ Saturated Fat: 5g
- ❖ Sodium: 520mg

Savor Morocco's rich and aromatic flavors from the comfort of your home. This chicken tagine dish, with its perfect blend of spices and textures, offers a delightful culinary journey, making your dinner unforgettable.

24: Garlic Roasted Chicken

Garlic-roasted chicken with lemon herbed seasoning is the epitome of homely comfort. This slow cooker dish will not only fill your kitchen with an aromatic allure but also satiate your tastebuds with its tender, flavorful bites.

Servings: 4

Prepping Time: 20 minutes

Cook Time: 4 hours

Difficulty: Easy

Ingredients:

> - 4 bone-in chicken breasts
> - 6 garlic cloves, minced
> - Zest and juice of 1 lemon
> - 2 tbsp olive oil
> - 1 tsp dried rosemary
> - 1 tsp dried thyme
> - Salt and pepper, to taste
> - Fresh parsley for garnish

Step-by-Step Preparation:

1. Combine garlic, lemon zest and juice, olive oil, rosemary, thyme, salt, and pepper in a bowl.
2. Rub the mixture generously over the chicken breasts.
3. Place the seasoned chicken into the slow cooker.
4. Cover and cook on low for 4 hours or until chicken is tender and fully cooked.
5. Once done, garnish with fresh parsley and serve hot.

Nutritional Facts: (Per serving)

- ❖ Calories: 320 kcal
- ❖ Protein: 34g
- ❖ Carbs: 4g
- ❖ Dietary Fiber: 1g
- ❖ Sugars: 1g
- ❖ Fat: 18g
- ❖ Saturated Fat: 4g
- ❖ Sodium: 320mg

With the elegance of fine dining and the simplicity of a home-cooked meal, this garlic-roasted chicken dish is perfect for busy weeknights or special occasions. Pair it with roasted veggies or a light salad, and you have a complete, nourishing meal ready to be relished.

25: Mushroom Beef Stroganoff

Succulent beef paired with aromatic mushrooms and a creamy sauce, this Mushroom Beef Stroganoff is a comforting delight, perfect for cool evenings. It is a classic dish elevated by the simplicity of a slow cooker, ensuring flavors meld seamlessly.

Servings: 6

Prepping Time: 20 minutes

Cook Time: 6 hours on low

Difficulty: Moderate

Ingredients:

- ➤ 2 lbs beef chuck, cut into 1-inch cubes
- ➤ 2 cups cremini mushrooms, sliced
- ➤ 2 cups champignons, sliced
- ➤ 1 large onion, diced
- ➤ 3 cloves garlic, minced
- ➤ 2 cups beef broth
- ➤ 1 cup sour cream
- ➤ 2 tbsp Worcestershire sauce

- ➢ Salt and pepper to taste
- ➢ 1 lb egg pasta
- ➢ 2 tbsp olive oil
- ➢ Fresh parsley, chopped (for garnish)

Step-by-Step Preparation:

1. Combine beef, mushrooms, onion, garlic, and broth in the slow cooker.
2. Season with salt, pepper, and Worcestershire sauce. Mix well.
3. Cover and cook on low for 5-6 hours or until beef is tender.
4. Boil egg pasta as per package instructions, then drain and set aside.
5. Before serving, stir sour cream into the beef mixture.
6. Serve stroganoff over egg pasta, drizzled with olive oil, and garnished with parsley.

Nutritional Facts: (Per serving)

- ❖ Calories: 580 kcal
- ❖ Protein: 32g
- ❖ Carbs: 45g
- ❖ Fat: 30g
- ❖ Dietary Fiber: 2g
- ❖ Sugars: 3g
- ❖ Sodium: 350mg

With the savory depth of mushrooms and tender chunks of beef, this Mushroom Beef Stroganoff serves as a quintessential comfort dish. The luscious creaminess and aroma from the slow-cooked concoction, paired with traditional egg pasta, will make your dinner time nothing short of exquisite. Enjoy this heartwarming meal with loved ones, and let the flavors take you on a delightful culinary journey.

26: Spicy Meatball Sub Sandwich

Dive into the rich flavors of this comforting dinner dish. The spicy meatballs paired with a tangy marinara sauce and melted cheese inside a crispy sub roll promise a meal that's sure to satisfy.

Servings: 4

Prepping Time: 20 minutes

Cook Time: 6 hours

Difficulty: Intermediate

Ingredients:

> - 500g ground beef or pork
> - 1 cup breadcrumbs
> - 1 egg, beaten
> - 2 tsp chili flakes
> - 1 tsp garlic powder
> - 2 cups marinara sauce
> - 4 sub rolls
> - 1 cup shredded mozzarella cheese
> - Fresh basil leaves for garnish

➤ Salt and pepper, to taste

Step-by-Step Preparation:

1. Combine ground meat, breadcrumbs, egg, chili flakes, garlic powder, salt, and pepper in a bowl. Mix well and form into meatballs.
2. Place meatballs at the bottom of the slow cooker.
3. Pour marinara sauce over the meatballs.
4. Cook on low for 6 hours.
5. Open the sub rolls and place meatballs inside. Top with marinara sauce and cheese.
6. Broil in an oven until the cheese melts.
7. Garnish with fresh basil leaves before serving.

Nutritional Facts: (Per serving)

❖ Calories: 580 kcal
❖ Protein: 32g
❖ Carbohydrates: 48g
❖ Fat: 28g
❖ Sodium: 980mg
❖ Sugar: 8g

After a long day, there's nothing like coming home to a flavorful and hearty sub sandwich simmering in the slow cooker. The combination of spicy meatballs, creamy cheese, and zesty marinara sauce enveloped in a toasted sub roll makes for an unforgettable meal experience.

27: Coq AU Vin

Indulge in the rich flavors of France with Coq au Vin, a classic dish blending chicken, bacon, mushrooms, and vegetables in a luscious red wine sauce. This slow cooker version captures the authentic taste with minimal effort, making it perfect for a gourmet dinner at home.

Servings: 4

Prepping Time: 20 minutes

Cook Time: 6 hours

Difficulty: Medium

Ingredients:

> - 4 bone-in, skin-on chicken thighs
> - 4 slices of bacon, chopped
> - 1 cup sliced mushrooms
> - 2 medium carrots, sliced
> - 1 onion, chopped
> - 3 cloves garlic, minced
> - 1 bottle (750 ml) red wine, preferably Burgundy
> - 2 cups chicken broth

- ➤ 2 bay leaves
- ➤ 1 tsp thyme
- ➤ 1 tbsp tomato paste
- ➤ Salt and pepper to taste
- ➤ 2 tbsp butter (for finishing)
- ➤ Fresh parsley (for garnish)

Step-by-Step Preparation:

1. In a skillet, cook the chopped bacon until crispy. Remove and set aside.
2. Brown chicken thighs in the bacon fat for about 3 minutes on each side.
3. Place chicken, bacon, mushrooms, carrots, onion, and garlic in the slow cooker.
4. Pour some wine into the skillet to deglaze, scraping the bits off the pan. Pour this and the rest of the wine, chicken broth, bay leaves, thyme, and tomato paste over the chicken.
5. Season with salt and pepper, then stir to mix.
6. Cook on low for 6 hours.
7. Before serving, remove the bay leaves and stir in the butter for a rich finish. Garnish with fresh parsley.

Nutritional Facts: (Per serving)

- ❖ Calories: 450
- ❖ Protein: 28g
- ❖ Fat: 20g
- ❖ Carbohydrates: 12g
- ❖ Fiber: 2g
- ❖ Sugars: 3g
- ❖ Sodium: 600mg

To experience France in your kitchen, dive into this hearty Coq au Vin. The tender chicken, rich wine sauce, and aromatic herbs will transport your taste buds straight to a rustic French bistro. Pair with crusty bread and enjoy this sumptuous, slow-cooked delicacy.

28: Jambalaya With Shrimps

A soulful blend of flavors, Jambalaya with shrimp and sausages is the quintessential comfort dish of the South. This dish melds savory sausages, succulent shrimp, and aromatic spices for a dinner that warms the heart.

Servings: 6

Prepping Time: 20 minutes

Cook Time: 4 hours

Difficulty: Easy

Ingredients:

- ➢ 500g medium shrimps, peeled and deveined
- ➢ 300g smoked sausage, sliced
- ➢ 1 cup uncooked long-grain rice
- ➢ 1 large onion, diced
- ➢ 1 green bell pepper, chopped
- ➢ 2 celery stalks, chopped
- ➢ 3 garlic cloves, minced
- ➢ 1 can (14 oz) diced tomatoes
- ➢ 1 tsp Cajun seasoning

- ➤ 1/2 tsp dried thyme
- ➤ 1/2 tsp paprika
- ➤ 2 cups chicken broth
- ➤ 2 green onions, chopped (for garnish)
- ➤ Salt and pepper to taste

Step-by-Step Preparation:

1. Combine the onion, bell pepper, celery, and garlic in your slow cooker.
2. Add the sliced sausages and uncooked rice.
3. Pour the diced tomatoes into chicken broth, then add the Cajun seasoning, thyme, paprika, salt, and pepper. Stir to mix well.
4. Cover and cook on LOW for 3-4 hours.
5. About 30 minutes before serving, stir in the shrimp.
6. Once the shrimp are pink and cooked through, your Jambalaya is ready. Garnish with green onions before serving.

Nutritional Facts: (Per serving)

- ❖ Calories: 350
- ❖ Protein: 28g
- ❖ Carbohydrates: 38g
- ❖ Fat: 10g
- ❖ Saturated Fat: 3g
- ❖ Cholesterol: 185mg
- ❖ Sodium: 950mg
- ❖ Fiber: 2g
- ❖ Sugar: 3g

Indulge in the rich, spicy undertones of this classic Southern dish. Perfect for cold evenings or gatherings, this Jambalaya with shrimp and sausages is a testament to the magic of slow-cooked flavors. Serve with crusty bread or a side salad, and let the symphony of tastes enchant your palate.

29: Asian Beef With Broccoli

Indulge in the savory fusion of tender beef and fresh broccoli, slow-cooked to perfection in an aromatic Asian sauce. This dish offers a burst of flavors, ensuring a delightful meal for the family.

Servings: 4

Prepping Time: 15 minutes

Cook Time: 4 hours on high or 6 hours on low

Difficulty: Easy

Ingredients:

> ➢ 1 lb beef chuck, thinly sliced
> ➢ 2 cups broccoli florets
> ➢ 1/4 cup low-sodium soy sauce
> ➢ 2 tbsp brown sugar
> ➢ 1 tbsp sesame oil
> ➢ 3 garlic cloves, minced
> ➢ 1 tsp grated ginger
> ➢ 2 tbsp cornstarch
> ➢ 1/4 cup water

Step-by-Step Preparation:

1. Whisk together soy sauce, brown sugar, sesame oil, garlic, and ginger in a bowl.
2. Place the beef slices into the slow cooker and pour the sauce.
3. Cook on high for 3-4 hours or low for 5-6 hours.
4. About 30 minutes before serving, whisk cornstarch and water until smooth. Stir into the slow cooker.
5. Add broccoli florets, stirring to coat them with the sauce.
6. Cook until broccoli is tender.
7. Serve over steamed rice or noodles.

Nutritional Facts: (Per serving)

- ❖ Calories: 320
- ❖ Protein: 26g
- ❖ Carbohydrates: 20g
- ❖ Dietary Fiber: 3g
- ❖ Sugars: 10g
- ❖ Fat: 15g
- ❖ Saturated Fat: 5g
- ❖ Cholesterol: 70mg
- ❖ Sodium: 550mg

End your day with this hearty Asian Beef with Broccoli, a flawless blend of rich tastes and textures. The ease of the slow cooker transforms simple ingredients into a gourmet meal, making dinner time effortless and enjoyable.

30: Creamy Tuscan Chicken

Experience the rich flavors of Tuscany in your kitchen with this creamy Tuscan chicken recipe. This slow cooker meal is a delightful combination of tastes and textures that will transport you straight to the heart of Italy.

Servings: 4-6 people

Prepping Time: 15 minutes

Cook Time: 4 hours on low

Difficulty: Easy

Ingredients:

- 4 boneless, skinless chicken breasts
- 1 cup heavy cream
- 1/2 cup grated parmesan cheese
- 1 cup fresh spinach, chopped
- 1/2 cup sun-dried tomatoes, chopped
- 3 garlic cloves, minced
- 1 tsp salt
- 1/2 tsp black pepper
- 1 tbsp olive oil

➤ 1/2 cup chicken broth

Step-by-Step Preparation:

1. In a slow cooker, place the chicken breasts at the bottom.
2. Mix heavy cream, parmesan, salt, and pepper in a bowl. Pour over the chicken.
3. Add in the sun-dried tomatoes, spinach, and minced garlic.
4. Drizzle olive oil and pour in chicken broth.
5. Cover and cook on low for 4 hours or until chicken is tender.
6. Serve hot, garnishing with additional parmesan if desired.

Nutritional Facts: (Per serving)

- ❖ Calories: 320
- ❖ Protein: 28g
- ❖ Carbs: 8g
- ❖ Fat: 20g
- ❖ Fiber: 2g
- ❖ Sugars: 3g

This Creamy Tuscan Chicken offers a gastronomic journey, capturing the essence of Tuscany's culinary traditions. It's the perfect dish for cozy dinners and gatherings, promising a feast for the palate and a symphony of flavors that resonates with the soul.

Chapter 4: Oceanside Seafood Wonders

31: Delicious Shrimp Alfredo

Savor the creamy goodness of shrimp Alfredo, intensified with a hint of garlic. This slow-cooked seafood delight promises a mouthwatering experience with every bite. Infused with flavors, it's perfect for weeknight dinners or special occasions.

Servings: 4

Prepping Time: 15 minutes

Cook Time: 4 hours

Difficulty: Medium

Ingredients:

> ➤ 1 lb large shrimp, peeled and deveined
> ➤ 1 cup heavy cream
> ➤ 3 cloves garlic, minced
> ➤ 1 cup grated Parmesan cheese
> ➤ 2 tbsp unsalted butter

- ➤ Salt and pepper to taste
- ➤ 12 oz fettuccine pasta
- ➤ Fresh parsley for garnish

Step-by-Step Preparation:

1. Add heavy cream, garlic, butter, salt, and pepper to the slow cooker. Stir to combine.
2. Cook on low for 3 hours.
3. Add shrimp and Parmesan cheese. Stir gently.
4. Continue cooking for another hour or until the shrimp is pink and fully cooked.
5. In a separate pot, boil pasta until al dente. Drain.
6. Pour the shrimp and Alfredo sauce over the pasta and garnish with fresh parsley.

Nutritional Facts: (Per serving)

- ❖ Calories: 600
- ❖ Protein: 35g
- ❖ Carbs: 55g
- ❖ Fat: 28g
- ❖ Cholesterol: 190mg
- ❖ Sodium: 600mg

Indulge in a plate of this heavenly shrimp Alfredo, a symphony of flavors harmonized perfectly with garlic and cream. Every forkful brings warmth and comfort. Perfect for cozy nights in or impressing a dinner guest. Enjoy!

32: New England Clam Chowder

Dive into the comforting flavors of the sea with this Creamy New England Clam Chowder. This dish is an effortless way to bring restaurant-quality soup straight to your table, perfectly garnished with oyster crackers.

Servings: 6

Prepping Time: 15 minutes

Cook Time: 4 hours on high or 6 hours on low

Difficulty: Easy

Ingredients:

> ➢ 2 cans (6.5 oz each) of chopped clams in juice
> ➢ 4 cups diced potatoes
> ➢ 1 cup diced onions
> ➢ 1 cup diced celery
> ➢ 2 cups heavy cream
> ➢ 4 cups clam juice or broth
> ➢ 3 garlic cloves, minced
> ➢ 1 teaspoon thyme
> ➢ 1 bay leaf

> ➤ 2 tablespoons unsalted butter
> ➤ Salt and pepper to taste
> ➤ Oyster crackers for garnish

Step-by-Step Preparation:

1. Combine potatoes, onions, celery, clam juice, garlic, thyme, and bay leaf in the slow cooker.
2. Cover and cook on low for 4-6 hours or until the vegetables are tender.
3. About 30 minutes before serving, add the clams, heavy cream, butter, salt, and pepper.
4. Stir well and continue cooking until heated through.
5. Serve in bowls and garnish with oyster crackers.

Nutritional Facts: (Per serving)

- ❖ Calories: 340
- ❖ Protein: 11g
- ❖ Fat: 23g
- ❖ Carbohydrates: 25g
- ❖ Sodium: 800mg
- ❖ Fiber: 3g
- ❖ Sugars: 3g

End your meal with this luxurious bowl of Clam Chowder, combining the rich taste of clams with the creaminess of the broth. Its velvety texture, paired with the crispness of oyster crackers, offers a delightful gastronomic experience perfect for chilly evenings.

33: Seafood Paella

Dive into the flavors of the coast with this Slow Cooker Seafood Paella. This authentic Spanish dish blends tender seafood with aromatic spices, delivering a culinary experience transporting you to a seaside cafe.

Servings: 4-6 people

Prepping Time: 20 minutes

Cook Time: 3 hours

Difficulty: Intermediate

Ingredients:

- 2 cups Arborio rice
- 1 lb. mixed seafood (shrimp, mussels, squid)
- 1/4 cup olive oil
- 1 onion, finely chopped
- 3 garlic cloves, minced
- 1 bell pepper, sliced
- 1/4 teaspoon saffron threads
- 1 teaspoon smoked paprika
- 1/2 teaspoon chili flakes

- ➢ 4 cups chicken or seafood broth
- ➢ 1/4 cup fresh parsley, chopped
- ➢ 1 lemon, sliced for garnish

Step-by-Step Preparation:

1. Heat olive oil and sauté onion and garlic until translucent in your slow cooker.
2. Add bell pepper and cook for another 2 minutes.
3. Stir in the rice, ensuring it's well coated with the oil.
4. Add saffron, paprika, chili flakes, and broth. Mix well.
5. Gently fold in the mixed seafood.
6. Set the slow cooker on low and cook for 3 hours or until rice is tender.
7. Garnish with fresh parsley and lemon slices before serving.

Nutritional Facts: (Per serving)

- ❖ Calories: 350
- ❖ Protein: 22g
- ❖ Carbohydrates: 50g
- ❖ Dietary Fiber: 2g
- ❖ Fats: 10g
- ❖ Sodium: 450mg

Savor the symphony of flavors in this delightful Slow Cooker Seafood Paella. A hearty meal that's both comforting and luxurious, it promises to be a favorite at any gathering, transporting your taste buds to the beaches of Spain with every bite. Enjoy!

34: Italian Risotto With Shrimps

Italian risotto with a rich medley of seafood, hailing from the heart of Italy, is a testament to the country's timeless culinary expertise. This slow-cooked masterpiece is a feast for the senses, bringing together succulent shrimp, mussels, octopus, clams, and sun-kissed tomatoes in an aromatic ensemble.

Servings: 4

Prepping Time: 20 minutes

Cook Time: 2 hours 30 minutes

Difficulty: Intermediate

Ingredients:

- ➢ 1 cup Arborio rice
- ➢ 2 tablespoons olive oil
- ➢ 1 medium onion, finely chopped
- ➢ 2 garlic cloves, minced
- ➢ 1/2 cup white wine
- ➢ 4 cups seafood broth
- ➢ 200g shrimps, peeled and deveined
- ➢ 150g mussels, cleaned

- ➤ 150g octopus, cleaned and cut into small pieces
- ➤ 150g clams, cleaned
- ➤ 2 ripe tomatoes, chopped
- ➤ 1/4 cup fresh parsley, chopped
- ➤ Salt and pepper to taste
- ➤ Zest of 1 lemon

Step-by-Step Preparation:

1. In the slow cooker, heat olive oil and sauté onions and garlic until translucent.
2. Add Arborio rice and stir for 2 minutes until it's well-coated with the oil.
3. Pour in white wine and let it simmer until reduced by half.
4. Add seafood broth, shrimp, mussels, octopus, and clams. Stir gently.
5. Set the slow cooker on low and let it cook for 2 hours.
6. 20 minutes before serving, add chopped tomatoes and season with salt, pepper, and lemon zest.
7. Once done, sprinkle with fresh parsley and serve hot.

Nutritional Facts: (Per serving)

- ❖ Calories: 420
- ❖ Protein: 25g
- ❖ Carbohydrates: 52g
- ❖ Dietary Fiber: 2g
- ❖ Sugars: 3g
- ❖ Fat: 10g
- ❖ Saturated Fat: 1.5g
- ❖ Cholesterol: 160mg
- ❖ Sodium: 800mg

In every spoonful of this Italian risotto, you'll be transported to a seaside trattoria, with waves crashing nearby and the aroma of the ocean in the air. The tenderness of the seafood, coupled with the creaminess of the risotto, makes for an unforgettable dish that embodies the spirit of Italian coastal cuisine.

35: Creamy Lobster Bisque

Indulge in a luxurious seafood treat with this slow cooker creamy lobster bisque, infused with the rich flavors of lobster meat, tomato paste, cream, and a splash of cognac. Perfect for special occasions or when you crave something extraordinary.

Servings: 6

Prepping Time: 20 minutes

Cook Time: 4 hours on low

Difficulty: Intermediate

Ingredients:

> 3 medium-sized lobster tails, cooked and meat removed
> 1 cup heavy cream
> 2 tablespoons tomato paste
> 1/4 cup cognac or brandy
> 1 onion, finely chopped
> 2 garlic cloves, minced
> 4 cups seafood or vegetable broth
> 2 tablespoons butter

- ➢ 2 tablespoons fresh parsley, chopped
- ➢ Salt and pepper to taste

Step-by-Step Preparation:

1. Combine lobster meat, onion, garlic, and broth in your slow cooker.
2. Stir in the tomato paste.
3. Cook on low for 3-4 hours, allowing flavors to meld.
4. 30 minutes before serving, stir in heavy cream and cognac.
5. Before serving, melt butter in a skillet, add parsley, and cook until fragrant. Stir this into the bisque.
6. Adjust seasoning with salt and pepper. Serve hot.

Nutritional Facts: (Per serving)

- ❖ Calories: 280
- ❖ Protein: 14g
- ❖ Carbohydrates: 5g
- ❖ Fat: 20g
- ❖ Cholesterol: 90mg
- ❖ Sodium: 540mg

Relish this lobster bisque's velvety texture and rich flavors, a culinary masterpiece from the deep. The slow cooker technique ensures a depth of flavor, making every spoonful a delightful experience. Pair with crusty bread and a glass of white wine for a complete gourmet experience.

36: Hot Coconut Prawn Soup

A warming bowl of Hot Coconut Prawn Soup is perfect for cozy nights. This slow-cooker seafood delight combines the richness of coconut with the spiciness of chili and aromatic curry to give your taste buds an unforgettable experience.

Servings: 4-6

Prepping Time: 15 minutes

Cook Time: 4 hours on low

Difficulty: Moderate

Ingredients:

- 500g fresh prawns, peeled and deveined
- 400ml can of coconut milk
- 1 large onion, finely chopped
- 3 garlic cloves, minced
- 2 red chilies, deseeded and finely chopped
- 2 tsp curry powder
- 2 tbsp fish sauce
- 1 lime, juiced

- ➢ Fresh coriander for garnishing
- ➢ Salt and pepper, to taste

Step-by-Step Preparation:

1. Combine onion, garlic, chilies, and curry powder in the slow cooker.
2. Pour in the coconut milk, fish sauce, and lime juice, stirring to mix.
3. Add the prawns, ensuring they are submerged in the mixture.
4. Set the slow cooker on low and cook for 4 hours.
5. Season with salt and pepper to taste.
6. Garnish with fresh coriander before serving.

Nutritional Facts: (Per serving)

- ❖ Calories: 280 kcal
- ❖ Protein: 20g
- ❖ Carbohydrates: 6g
- ❖ Fat: 20g
- ❖ Saturated Fat: 15g
- ❖ Sodium: 850mg
- ❖ Fiber: 1g
- ❖ Sugar: 2g

Indulge in the comforting layers of flavors from this Hot Coconut Prawn Soup. The beauty of slow cooking melds all the ingredients, creating a harmonious blend of taste and aroma. Whether it's a chilly evening or a desire for hearty seafood soup, this dish is your perfect bowl of comfort.

37: Salmon Teriyaki Over Vegetables

Savor the flavors of the sea and the Orient with our Salmon Teriyaki over vegetables slow-cooked to perfection. This heart-healthy seafood dish marries rich salmon with a sweet and savory glaze over a bed of crunchy veggies. Perfect for family dinners or sophisticated soirees.

Servings: 4

Prepping Time: 20 minutes

Cook Time: 4 hours on low

Difficulty: Easy

Ingredients:

- ➤ 4 salmon fillets
- ➤ 1/2 cup teriyaki sauce
- ➤ 1 tablespoon honey
- ➤ 1 tablespoon minced garlic
- ➤ 1 teaspoon ginger, grated
- ➤ 2 cups mixed vegetables (broccoli, bell peppers, snap peas)
- ➤ 1 tablespoon sesame oil
- ➤ Salt and pepper, to taste

- ➢ 1 tablespoon sesame seeds (for garnish)
- ➢ Sliced green onions (for garnish)

Step-by-Step Preparation:

1. Whisk together teriyaki sauce, honey, garlic, and ginger in a bowl.
2. Place the mixed vegetables at the bottom of the slow cooker and drizzle with sesame oil.
3. Season salmon fillets with salt and pepper, then place them on the vegetables.
4. Pour the teriyaki mixture over the salmon.
5. Cover and cook on low for 4 hours.
6. Serve hot, garnished with sesame seeds and green onions.

Nutritional Facts: (Per serving)

- ❖ Calories: 350
- ❖ Protein: 34g
- ❖ Carbohydrates: 18g
- ❖ Dietary Fiber: 3g
- ❖ Sugars: 12g
- ❖ Fat: 16g
- ❖ Saturated Fat: 3g
- ❖ Cholesterol: 75mg
- ❖ Sodium: 920mg

This Salmon Teriyaki over vegetables is a seamless blend of Japanese flair with the nutritious benefits of fresh seafood and vegetables. Served straight from the slow cooker, each bite promises warmth, flavor, and an unforgettable culinary experience. Dive into this dish and let your taste buds sail!

38: Seafood Gumbo

Warm up your soul with this tantalizing slow-cooker seafood gumbo. Packed with a medley of marine delights and rich flavors, it's a Southern favorite that will impress any seafood lover.

Servings: 6-8

Prepping Time: 25 minutes

Cook Time: 4 hours on high, 8 hours on low

Difficulty: Intermediate

Ingredients:

- 1 cup okra, sliced
- 1 cup onion, chopped
- 1 bell pepper, chopped
- 2 cloves garlic, minced
- 1 can (14 oz.) diced tomatoes
- 1 lb shrimp, peeled and deveined
- 1/2 lb crab meat
- 1/2 lb andouille sausage, sliced
- 2 bay leaves

- ➢ 2 tsp Creole seasoning
- ➢ 1 tsp thyme
- ➢ 1 tsp paprika
- ➢ 4 cups chicken or seafood broth
- ➢ Salt and pepper, to taste
- ➢ 2 tbsp olive oil
- ➢ Fresh parsley for garnish

Step-by-Step Preparation:

1. In a skillet, heat olive oil and sauté onions, bell pepper, garlic, and okra until tender.
2. Transfer the sautéed vegetables to the slow cooker.
3. Add tomatoes, broth, bay leaves, Creole seasoning, thyme, paprika, salt, and pepper. Stir well.
4. Add in the sausage slices.
5. Cover and cook on low for 7 hours or high for 3 hours.
6. Add shrimp and crab meat in the last hour of cooking.
7. Once cooked, remove bay leaves and garnish with fresh parsley. Serve hot with rice.

Nutritional Facts: (Per serving)

- ❖ Calories: 320
- ❖ Protein: 25g
- ❖ Carbohydrates: 14g
- ❖ Dietary Fiber: 3g
- ❖ Total Fat: 18g
- ❖ Saturated Fat: 5g
- ❖ Cholesterol: 150mg
- ❖ Sodium: 950mg

From the heart of the bayou to your dinner table, this seafood gumbo offers a mouthful of coastal bliss. The slow-cooked medley of flavors melds beautifully, creating a hearty and indulgent dish. This gumbo will be a hit, whether it's a cozy weekend meal or a festive gathering.

39: Steamed Crabs

Indulge in the coastal flavors of steamed crabs elevated with a zesty dipping sauce. This slow cooker recipe ensures perfectly cooked crabs every time, paired beautifully with a spicy kick.

Servings: 4

Prepping Time: 15 minutes

Cook Time: 2 hours

Difficulty: Intermediate

Ingredients:

- ➤ 4 giant fresh crabs, cleaned and quartered
- ➤ 2 cups water
- ➤ 1 tablespoon salt
- ➤ 2 cloves garlic, minced
- ➤ 1/2 cup soy sauce
- ➤ 2 tablespoons chili paste
- ➤ 1 tablespoon lime juice
- ➤ 1 teaspoon sugar
- ➤ 2 green onions, chopped

Step-by-Step Preparation:

1. Place crabs in the slow cooker.
2. Mix water and salt in a bowl until dissolved and pour over the crabs.
3. Set the slow cooker on low and cook for 2 hours.
4. Combine garlic, soy sauce, chili paste, lime juice, sugar, and green onions in a separate bowl to create the dipping sauce.
5. Once the crabs are done, serve immediately with the spicy dipping sauce on the side.

Nutritional Facts: (Per serving)

- ❖ Calories: 210
- ❖ Protein: 22g
- ❖ Carbs: 6g
- ❖ Fats: 10g
- ❖ Sodium: 1290mg
- ❖ Sugar: 2g

Embark on a flavorful journey with the delightful blend of tender crabs and spicy sauce. This slow cooker delicacy brings the taste of the seaside to your table, promising an unforgettable dining experience. Perfect for special occasions or whenever you crave a touch of the ocean's bounty.

40: Stuffed Squid With Tomato Sauce

Transport your taste buds to the coast with this savory, slow-cooked seafood dish. The succulent squid, filled with fresh vegetables, bathes in a rich tomato sauce, delivering an exquisite blend of flavors and textures.

Servings: 4

Prepping Time: 30 minutes

Cook Time: 3 hours

Difficulty: Moderate

Ingredients:

- ➤ 4 medium-sized squids, cleaned and tentacles removed
- ➤ 1 cup diced bell peppers (red and yellow)
- ➤ 1 onion, finely chopped
- ➤ 2 garlic cloves, minced
- ➤ 1 cup breadcrumbs
- ➤ 1/4 cup chopped fresh parsley
- ➤ 2 cups tomato sauce
- ➤ 1/4 cup white wine (optional)
- ➤ 1 tsp olive oil

➤ Salt and pepper to taste

Step-by-Step Preparation:

1. Mix bell peppers, onion, garlic, breadcrumbs, and parsley in a bowl. Season with salt and pepper.
2. Stuff each squid with the vegetable mixture.
3. In a slow cooker, pour tomato sauce, olive oil, and white wine.
4. Place the stuffed squids in the sauce.
5. Cover and cook on low for 3 hours until squids are tender.
6. Serve warm, drizzled with the tomato sauce from the cooker.

Nutritional Facts: (Per serving)

❖ Calories: 240
❖ Protein: 18g
❖ Carbohydrates: 26g
❖ Fat: 5g
❖ Fiber: 3g
❖ Sodium: 370mg

Indulge in a marine culinary adventure without ever leaving home. Each bite of this delectable dish, with its harmonious play of flavors, promises a gastronomic journey. Whether shared with loved ones or savored solo, this stuffed squid recipe is a testament to the ocean's bounties and the magic of slow cooking.

Chapter 5: Soulful Soup Soirees

41: Chicken Tortilla Soup

Warm up with a bowl of flavorful Chicken Tortilla Soup, effortlessly cooked in a slow cooker. This hearty soup combines tender chicken, beans, and veggies with spice to warm your soul.

Servings: 6

Prepping Time: 15 minutes

Cook Time: 6 hours

Difficulty: Easy

Ingredients:

- ➤ 2 chicken breasts, boneless and skinless
- ➤ 1 can (15 oz) black beans, rinsed and drained
- ➤ 1 can (15 oz) corn, drained
- ➤ 1 can (10 oz) diced tomatoes with green chilis
- ➤ 4 cups chicken broth
- ➤ 1 medium onion, chopped

- ➢ 2 cloves garlic, minced
- ➢ 1 tsp ground cumin
- ➢ 1 tsp chili powder
- ➢ Salt and pepper to taste
- ➢ 1 cup tortilla strips
- ➢ Fresh cilantro and lime wedges for garnish

Step-by-Step Preparation:

1. Place chicken breasts at the bottom of the slow cooker.
2. Add black beans, corn, diced tomatoes, onion, and garlic.
3. Pour chicken broth and season with cumin, chili powder, salt, and pepper.
4. Set the slow cooker to low and cook for 6 hours.
5. After 6 hours, shred the chicken inside the slow cooker using two forks.
6. Serve in bowls, garnishing with tortilla strips, cilantro, and a squeeze of lime.

Nutritional Facts: (Per serving):

- ❖ Calories: 280
- ❖ Protein: 24g
- ❖ Carbohydrates: 35g
- ❖ Fat: 5g
- ❖ Fiber: 7g
- ❖ Sodium: 650mg

Warm flavors, tender chicken, and a hint of spice make this Chicken Tortilla Soup the perfect comfort meal. Whether enjoyed with loved ones or savored alone, it will become a staple in your repertoire.

42: Chicken Noodle Soup

Warm your soul with a classic comfort dish, Chicken noodle soup with carrots and dill. This heartwarming recipe combines the rich flavors of chicken with the zest of dill and the sweet bite of carrots.

Servings: 6

Prepping Time: 15 minutes

Cook Time: 4-6 hours on low

Difficulty: Easy

Ingredients:

- ➢ 2 boneless, skinless chicken breasts
- ➢ 8 cups chicken broth
- ➢ 2 cups carrots, sliced
- ➢ 1 cup celery, chopped
- ➢ 1 onion, diced
- ➢ 2 garlic cloves, minced
- ➢ 1 cup egg noodles
- ➢ 3 tbsp fresh dill, chopped
- ➢ Salt and pepper to taste

Step-by-Step Preparation:

1. Place chicken breasts, carrots, celery, onion, and garlic in the slow cooker.
2. Pour chicken broth over the ingredients.
3. Cover and cook on low for 4-6 hours until chicken is tender.
4. Approximately 30 minutes before serving, add in the egg noodles.
5. Once the noodles are tender, shred the chicken using two forks and return to the soup.
6. Stir in the fresh dill and season with salt and pepper.
7. Serve hot and enjoy.

Nutritional Facts: (Per serving)

- ❖ Calories: 220
- ❖ Protein: 20g
- ❖ Carbohydrates: 18g
- ❖ Dietary Fiber: 2g
- ❖ Sugars: 3g
- ❖ Fat: 6g
- ❖ Cholesterol: 55mg
- ❖ Sodium: 890mg

This Chicken noodle soup with carrots and dill is perfect for chilly nights. With the ease of the slow cooker doing most of the work, you can savor a bowlful of nostalgic flavors and warmth. Remember a crusty loaf of bread on the side for a complete, cozy experience.

43: Creamy Broccoli Cheese Soup

Delight your palate with a delectable broccoli, cheese, and spices blend. This spicy, thick, creamy broccoli cheese soup is a comforting bowl of warmth, perfect for chilly nights.

Servings: 4

Prepping Time: 15 minutes

Cook Time: 4 hours (slow cooker)

Difficulty: Easy

Ingredients:

- 4 cups fresh broccoli, chopped
- 1 onion, finely chopped
- 3 cups cheddar cheese, grated
- 2 cups heavy cream
- 1 tsp red pepper flakes
- 4 cups chicken or vegetable broth
- 3 garlic cloves, minced
- Salt and pepper, to taste

Step-by-Step Preparation:

1. Place chopped broccoli, onion, and garlic in the slow cooker.
2. Pour in the chicken or vegetable broth.
3. Cook on low for 3 hours.
4. Stir in heavy cream, grated cheese, red pepper flakes, salt, and pepper.
5. Cook on low for an additional hour or until soup thickens.
6. Blend the soup with an immersion blender for a creamy texture.
7. Serve hot and enjoy!

Nutritional Facts: (Per serving)

- ❖ Calories: 540 kcal
- ❖ Protein: 18g
- ❖ Fat: 45g
- ❖ Carbohydrates: 18g
- ❖ Fiber: 4g
- ❖ Sugar: 5g

This broccoli cheese soup is a real treat for those who love the harmony of heat and creaminess. Its rich texture and robust flavors make it a staple in your culinary repertoire. Serve with crusty bread for a full, satisfying meal. Enjoy!

44: Black Bean Thick Soup

Dive into the heartwarming world of slow-cooked soups with this spicy and flavorful Black Bean Thick Soup infused with chili peppers. This dish is nourishing and packs a punch, making it perfect for those chilly evenings or when you're in the mood for something with a kick.

Servings: 4

Prepping Time: 20 minutes

Cook Time: 6 hours

Difficulty: Easy

Ingredients:

> 2 cups dried black beans, soaked overnight
> 4 cups vegetable broth
> 2 medium-sized chili peppers, finely chopped
> 1 large onion, chopped
> 3 cloves garlic, minced
> 1 teaspoon cumin powder
> 1 teaspoon paprika
> Salt and pepper, to taste

➢ Fresh cilantro for garnish
➢ 1 lime, cut into wedges

Step-by-Step Preparation:

1. Combine soaked black beans, vegetable broth, chili peppers, onion, and garlic in a slow cooker.
2. Stir in cumin, paprika, salt, and pepper.
3. Cover and cook on low for 6 hours or until beans are tender.
4. Once done, use an immersion blender to slightly puree some of the beans, leaving it thick but with some beans whole.
5. Serve hot, garnished with fresh cilantro and a wedge of lime.

Nutritional Facts: (Per serving)

❖ Calories: 280 kcal
❖ Protein: 15g
❖ Carbohydrates: 53g
❖ Dietary Fiber: 13g
❖ Fats: 2g
❖ Sodium: 450mg

This Black Bean Thick Soup is rich in flavor and has nutritional benefits. The slow-cooked beans render a velvety texture, harmonizing with the zest from the chili peppers. Pair it with some crusty bread for a satisfying meal, or enjoy it as a spicy, comforting bowl of goodness.

45: Coconut Milk Soup With Chicken

Infused with aromatic spices and tender chicken, this Coconut Milk Soup offers a comforting embrace in every spoonful. Perfect for a cozy dinner, the slow cooker does all the hard work for you.

Servings: 4

Prepping Time: 15 minutes

Cook Time: 4 hours on low

Difficulty: Easy

Ingredients:

> - 2 boneless chicken breasts, cubed
> - 1 can (400ml) coconut milk
> - 4 cups chicken broth
> - 2 stalks lemongrass, finely chopped
> - 1-inch ginger, sliced
> - 2 cloves garlic, minced
> - 2 red chillies, sliced (optional)
> - 1 tbsp fish sauce
> - 1 tsp sugar

- ➤ Salt, to taste
- ➤ Fresh cilantro and lime wedges for garnish

Step-by-Step Preparation:

1. Place chicken, coconut milk, broth, lemongrass, ginger, garlic, and chilies into the slow cooker.
2. Stir in fish sauce, sugar, and salt.
3. Cover and cook on low for 4 hours.
4. Once done, taste and adjust the seasoning if needed.
5. Serve hot, garnished with fresh cilantro and lime wedges.

Nutritional Facts: (Per serving)

- ❖ Calories: 340
- ❖ Protein: 28g
- ❖ Carbohydrates: 10g
- ❖ Fat: 22g
- ❖ Sodium: 800mg
- ❖ Fiber: 2g
- ❖ Sugar: 3g

The fusion of silky coconut milk, fragrant spices, and succulent chicken creates a rich and flavorful experience. This Coconut Milk Soup With Chicken is perfect for any weather and invites you to indulge in a bowl of warmth and delight.

46: Tomato Soup With Basil

Dive into the comforting embrace of this Tomato Soup with Basil. Perfectly capturing the essence of home-cooked goodness, this slow cooker soup is a delightful infusion of tangy tomatoes and aromatic basil, ensuring every spoonful treats your taste buds.

Servings: 4

Prepping Time: 15 minutes

Cook Time: 4 hours on low

Difficulty: Easy

Ingredients:

- ➢ 6 ripe tomatoes, diced
- ➢ 1 onion, finely chopped
- ➢ 3 cloves garlic, minced
- ➢ 1/4 cup fresh basil leaves, chopped
- ➢ 2 cups vegetable broth
- ➢ 1 tsp sugar
- ➢ Salt and pepper to taste
- ➢ 1/2 cup heavy cream (optional)

➢ 2 tbsp olive oil

Step-by-Step Preparation:

1. Combine tomatoes, onion, garlic, basil, and vegetable broth in your slow cooker.
2. Add sugar, salt, and pepper.
3. Drizzle olive oil over the mixture.
4. Cover and cook on low for 4 hours.
5. After 4 hours, blend the soup using a hand blender until smooth.
6. If desired, stir in the heavy cream for a creamier texture.
7. Serve hot, garnished with some fresh basil leaves.

Nutritional Facts: (Per serving)

❖ Calories: 150
❖ Protein: 2g
❖ Carbohydrates: 18g
❖ Dietary Fiber: 3g
❖ Sugars: 10g
❖ Fat: 8g
❖ Sodium: 500mg

This Tomato Soup with Basil is more than just a meal; it's an experience. Its creamy texture and authentic flavors promise a nostalgic journey to those cherished memories of family dinners. Pair it with some crusty bread for the perfect cozy meal. Enjoy!

47: Onion Soup

Warm up with this savory slow-cooker onion soup. This recipe is perfect for chilly evenings or when craving a hearty soup that comforts the belly and the soul.

Servings: 4-6 people

Prepping Time: 20 minutes

Cook Time: 6 hours

Difficulty: Easy

Ingredients:

- 6 large onions, thinly sliced
- 4 cups beef broth
- 2 cups water
- 1/2 cup dry white wine (optional)
- 2 garlic cloves, minced
- 2 bay leaves
- 1 tsp dried thyme
- 1 tsp salt
- 1/2 tsp black pepper

- ➢ 4 slices of toasted French bread
- ➢ 1 cup grated Gruyère cheese

Step-by-Step Preparation:

1. Place sliced onions into the slow cooker.
2. Add beef broth, water, white wine, garlic, bay leaves, thyme, salt, and pepper.
3. Cover and cook on low for 6 hours.
4. Discard the bay leaves.
5. To serve, ladle the soup into bowls, top with a slice of toasted French bread, and sprinkle with Gruyère cheese.

Nutritional Facts: (Per serving)

- ❖ Calories: 280
- ❖ Carbohydrates: 30g
- ❖ Protein: 15g
- ❖ Fat: 10g
- ❖ Sodium: 860mg
- ❖ Fiber: 4g
- ❖ Sugars: 8g

Savor every spoonful of this decadent onion soup. Slow-cooked to perfection, its depth of flavor makes every bite a delicious experience. Pair it with a crisp salad or crusty bread for a meal that satisfies and delights. This soup will surely warm your heart whether you're sharing with family or enjoying a quiet moment alone.

48: Moroccan Sweet Potato Lentil Soup

Moroccan Sweet Potato Lentil Soup is a nourishing blend of flavors, fusing sweet potatoes and lentils with aromatic spices. This slow cooker delicacy is ideal for cooler evenings and promises a burst of warmth and comfort.

Servings: 6

Prepping Time: 20 minutes

Cook Time: 6-8 hours

Difficulty: Easy

Ingredients:

- 2 large sweet potatoes, peeled and diced
- 1 cup dried lentils, rinsed and drained
- 1 large onion, finely chopped
- 3 cloves garlic, minced
- 1 tsp ground cumin
- 1 tsp ground coriander
- 1/2 tsp ground cinnamon
- 1/4 tsp ground turmeric
- 1/4 tsp cayenne pepper

- ➤ 6 cups vegetable broth
- ➤ Salt and pepper to taste
- ➤ Fresh herbs (like cilantro or parsley) for garnish

Step-by-Step Preparation:

1. Place sweet potatoes, lentils, onion, and garlic in the slow cooker.
2. Sprinkle in the spices: cumin, coriander, cinnamon, turmeric, and cayenne pepper.
3. Pour in the vegetable broth and stir to mix.
4. Set the slow cooker to low and cook for 6-8 hours or until lentils and potatoes are tender.
5. Season with salt and pepper to taste.
6. Serve hot and garnish with freshly chopped herbs.

Nutritional Facts: (Per serving)

- ❖ Calories: 210
- ❖ Protein: 12g
- ❖ Carbohydrates: 45g
- ❖ Dietary Fiber: 7g
- ❖ Sugars: 6g
- ❖ Fat: 1g
- ❖ Sodium: 520mg

Dive into a bowl of this Moroccan delight, and let the flavors transport you to the bustling streets of Marrakech. The vibrant herbs add a pop of color and a freshness that balances the soup's richness. Perfect for sharing with loved ones on a chilly evening.

49: White Bean Soup With Parsley

On chilly days, there's nothing more heartwarming than a bowl of hearty soup. This white bean soup with parsley promises a comforting blend of flavors that is both nourishing and flavorful. Perfect for those who crave simplicity with a touch of elegance in their meals.

Servings: 6

Prepping Time: 15 minutes

Cook Time: 6 hours on low

Difficulty: Easy

Ingredients:

> ➢ 2 cups dried white beans, soaked overnight
> ➢ 1 large onion, diced
> ➢ 3 garlic cloves, minced
> ➢ 1 cup fresh parsley, finely chopped
> ➢ 1 carrot, diced
> ➢ 1 celery stalk, diced
> ➢ 6 cups vegetable broth
> ➢ 1 tsp salt

- ➢ 1/2 tsp black pepper
- ➢ 1 bay leaf

Step-by-Step Preparation:

1. Drain the soaked beans and rinse them under cold water.
2. Place beans, onion, garlic, carrot, and celery in the slow cooker.
3. Add the vegetable broth, salt, pepper, and bay leaf.
4. Cook on low for 6 hours.
5. About 30 minutes before serving, add the chopped parsley.
6. Before serving, remove the bay leaf and season with additional salt and pepper if needed.

Nutritional Facts: (Per serving)

- ❖ Calories: 210
- ❖ Protein: 12g
- ❖ Fat: 1g
- ❖ Carbohydrates: 40g
- ❖ Fiber: 10g
- ❖ Sodium: 700mg

Indulge in this timeless classic, ensuring a nourishing experience in every spoonful. The soft beans and aromatic parsley make it a soup to remember. Pair it with crusty bread, and let this soup bring warmth and delight to your table.

50: Split Pea Soup

Savor the comforting flavors of this classic Split Pea Soup with Chunks of Ham, ideal for chilly evenings. This recipe combines simplicity with hearty ingredients, making it perfect for family dinners or meal prep.

Servings: 6

Prepping Time: 15 minutes

Cook Time: 6-8 hours on low

Difficulty: Easy

Ingredients:

> - 1 lb dried split peas, rinsed and drained
> - 2 cups diced ham
> - 1 large onion, chopped
> - 3 carrots, peeled and diced
> - 2 celery stalks, chopped
> - 4 cloves garlic, minced
> - 1 bay leaf
> - 6 cups chicken broth
> - Salt and pepper, to taste

Step-by-Step Preparation:

1. The slow cooker combines split peas, ham, onion, carrots, celery, garlic, and bay leaf.
2. Pour in the chicken broth, ensuring that all ingredients are covered.
3. Cook on low for 6-8 hours or until peas are soft and soup has thickened.
4. Before serving, season with salt and pepper to taste and remove the bay leaf.
5. Ladle into bowls and serve warm.

Nutritional Facts: (Per serving)

- ❖ Calories: 350
- ❖ Protein: 25g
- ❖ Carbohydrates: 45g
- ❖ Dietary Fiber: 16g
- ❖ Sugars: 8g
- ❖ Fat: 5g
- ❖ Saturated Fat: 1.5g
- ❖ Sodium: 900mg

Relish the comfort of homemade Split Pea Soup with Ham, perfect for warming up from the inside out. The slow cooker does the heavy lifting, letting the flavors meld to perfection. Pair with crusty bread for a meal that satisfies both hunger and the soul.

Conclusion

As we wrap up this delightful culinary journey through "Made Easy Slow Cooker Recipes," I hope that Olivia Anderson's passion for cooking has inspired you to venture further into slow-cooked meals. With every page turned and every recipe tried, you've embarked on an adventure that has expanded your culinary repertoire while providing delicious and fuss-free dinners to enjoy with your loved ones.

This book shows you that slow cooker recipes extend far beyond basic stews and soups. Our carefully curated selection offers a delightful mix of traditional favorites, innovative reimaginations, and global flavors, all brimming with decadent tastes and comforting textures. Whether you're feeding a crowd, preparing for the week, or cooking for a quiet night in, these recipes will serve your needs.

We offer our utmost gratitude for your support and trust in this journey. We hope this collection has filled your tables with great meals and your hearts with the joy of cooking. Remember, the magic of slow cooking lies in the mingling of flavors over time, resulting in mouthwatering dishes that speak volumes of love and care.

In closing, it doesn't matter if you're a novice home cook or a seasoned chef; there's always room at the table for good food and good company. Here's to a future filled with scrumptious slow-cooked meals. Happy cooking!

Printed in Great Britain
by Amazon

38608309R00059